THE
GROSSEST ANIMAL
FACTS EVER
Book for Kids

WONDERFUL WORLD OF ANIMALS BOOK 5

JACK LEWIS

The Grossest Animal Facts Ever Book for Kids
Wonderful World of Animals Book 5
Copyright © 2023 by Starry Dreamer Publishing

For information contact:
Starry Dreamer Publishing LLC
1603 Capitol Ave. Suite 310 A377
Cheyenne, Wyoming 82001
starrydreamerpub@gmail.com

Written by Jack Lewis
Photo Credits: All images contained herein are used under license from Shutterstock.com, Pixabay.com and Creative Commons (See Index for complete list)
Front Cover Photo Credits:
Andy Crocker/Shutterstock, Wallace Keck NPS
Back Cover Photo Credits:
Ajit S N, Ian Fox/Shutterstock

ISBN: 978-1-961492-07-3 (Hardcover) 978-1-961492-05-9 (Paperback)

Library of Congress Control Number: 2023924514
First Edition: January 2024

STARRY DREAMER PUBLISHING

Fulmar

North Atlantic, North Pacific, and Alaska

At first glance, the fulmar looks like a normal seabird, kind of like a seagull. These birds live in parts of the North Atlantic, North Pacific, and Alaska. But fulmars have a nasty defense trick that makes them anything but normal! When threatened, they barf up a jet of stinky, oily liquid! The name "fulmar" even comes from the phrase "foul gull."

Fulmar chicks will happily squirt this gross oil if their nest is bothered. The smell makes most four-legged predators turn around and run away! But for other birds, getting sprayed can be deadly. The sticky oil glues their feathers together so they can't fly. Many get stuck and fall into the ocean.

No other bird has a built-in oil tank just for grossing out enemies!

Anateris Scorpion

South America

When attacked, some animals fight back. Others run away. But the Ananteris scorpion does something gross - it cracks its tail off!

These little South American scorpions can detach part of their tail to escape predators. Here's the icky part: their anus is right near the stinger at the tail's end. So breaking their tail means losing the ability to poop!

Without a tail for pooping, the scorpion gets badly constipated. Over months, waste builds up and blocks its tiny gut until the scorpion bloats up and dies. That's one brutal consequence of blasting your butt off!

EWWW... WHY DO ANIMALS DO THAT?!

As humans, we're quick to label things as gross, nasty, or disgusting. But in nature, there's a reason for everything, and there's no such thing as something being unnecessarily gross. Even animals and insects we consider yucky, slimy, or creepy crawly are just living creatures trying to survive. Their so-called disgusting traits - be it oozy slime, terrible stink, or bizarre features - serve an important purpose in their ability to thrive. What seems sickening and weird to us is actually useful and normal for them.

So next time you see a creature that makes your nose scrunch and your skin crawl, try to have an open mind. Remember, in the natural world, everything has its place and purpose, no matter how downright gross it may appear to our human sensibilities! We can still respect and appreciate even the ickiest, gooiest, grossest members of the animal kingdom.

ICKY FACT:

Wombats poop cubes to save space! Their square scat stacks neatly, so more fits in their guts.

Horsehair Worm

South America

Horsehair worms are disturbing parasites named for their long, thin bodies that tangle together like hair. These wiggly worms start out tiny as larvae in freshwater. If swallowed by insects like crickets and beetles, the larvae grow rapidly inside their hosts by intricate coiling and consuming nutrients from body fluids and fat stores. After developing into adults up to 3 feet long, the worms manipulate the host's brain, causing the insect to leap into water. There, the enormous worm erupts and swims away while the host dies. The worms mate in the water, the females lay eggs that hatch into larvae, and the freaky cycle repeats. **How crazy is that?**

With their brain-controlling, host-bursting, tangled lifestyle, horsehair worms earn their awful reputation!

Jackal

Africa, Asia, and Europe

Jackals are wild scavengers that never waste a scrap of food. These canines gulp down leftover carcasses that even lions couldn't finish. They'll chomp on a disease-ridden body that's been rotting in the hot sun for days! When lions leave scraps behind, jackals happily slurp up whatever's left on the bony plate. For jackals, no scrap of meat goes uneaten - even if it's rotten or regurgitated. Regarding snack time, these wild canines have zero standards and zero waste!

Jackals feed their pups by barfing up partially digested food. If the pups can't finish it all, no problem – the adults just re-eat their own vomit meal again!

Hagfish

Northwest Pacific Ocean

Hagfish are super slimy eel-like sea creatures. Their tentacles on their heads give them a Medusa-like appearance. Hagfish use those tentacles to burrow deep into dead carcasses on the ocean floor. Once inside, they devour the carcass from the inside out! As they eat, hagfish secrete tons of slime from their bodies. This slippery goo chokes other scavengers trying to eat the same carcass. Sometimes, hagfish tie themselves in knots to scrape the goo off their bodies and then feed on the slime! If attacked, they can cover predators with gallons of nasty slime, too.

These unforgettable fish are slime factories!

Usually, a hagfish only lets out a tiny bit of slime, less than a teaspoon, from the 100 slime glands along its body. But crazy fast - in less than half a second - that little bit of goo expands by 10,000 times! That's enough stinky hagfish slime to fill up a big bucket!

Xenomorph Wasp

Australia

Have you ever seen the movie Alien? The alien creature Xenomorph injects its baby into an astronaut's body. A few days later...BAM! The baby alien bursts out of the poor guy's chest. Gross! Well, a scientist in Australia found a wasp that does something similar - it injects its eggs into victims like moth caterpillars. As the eggs grow inside the caterpillar, they eat its insides until they pop out as full larva babies! It gets even crazier. Sometimes, the caterpillar survives like a zombie, forced to protect the larva cocoon until they hatch into wasps.

Since the scientist was a sci-fi fan, he named the wasp *Dolichogenidea xenomorph* after the Alien movies. This real-life wasp is as nasty as the fictional Xenomorph, bursting out of bodies!

ICKY FACT:

Penguin pee makes up 3% of Antarctic ice! So, next time you're in Antarctica, remember not to lick those glaciers!

Oxpecker

Africa

Oxpeckers are tiny birds that ride around on large animals like rhinos and giraffes to get a free meal. They pick ticks, dead skin, and gunk off their huge hosts - it's an all-you-can-eat bug and gunk buffet! These birds get their beaks way deep into every nook and cranny, slurping up anything they can find.

There's a dark side too. Oxpeckers don't just clean their hosts - they also chew open wounds to drink blood! Research shows they actually slow down healing because they can't stop pecking at scabs. That's right - oxpeckers linger over injuries like vampires, making the wounds worse. Their relationship is part helpful and part parasite. When the gunk grooming turns to blood slurping, their animal hosts probably wish these gnarly birds would bug off!

Gross as they are, Oxpeckers have helped endangered black rhinos survive. When they hear hunters, oxpeckers hiss a loud warning for their vision-challenged hosts to run.

Leech

Across the World

Leeches are creepy little creatures that love to suck blood. They hang out in lakes or rainforests, waiting to latch onto warm-blooded animals. With their three sharp jaws, they bite into the skin and slurp up the blood. Some leeches even have special spit that makes the bites numb, so the animals don't feel a thing! After a big blood feast, leeches take a break, storing extra blood in their bodies for later. But if they don't find more blood soon, they can get really hungry and shrivel up. And if one overfeeds too quickly, it might burst open, spraying blood everywhere! *YUCK!*

ICKY FACT:

The Siberian chipmunk smells like the toilet on purpose! Siberian chipmunks coat themselves in any snake pee they find to scare away enemies.

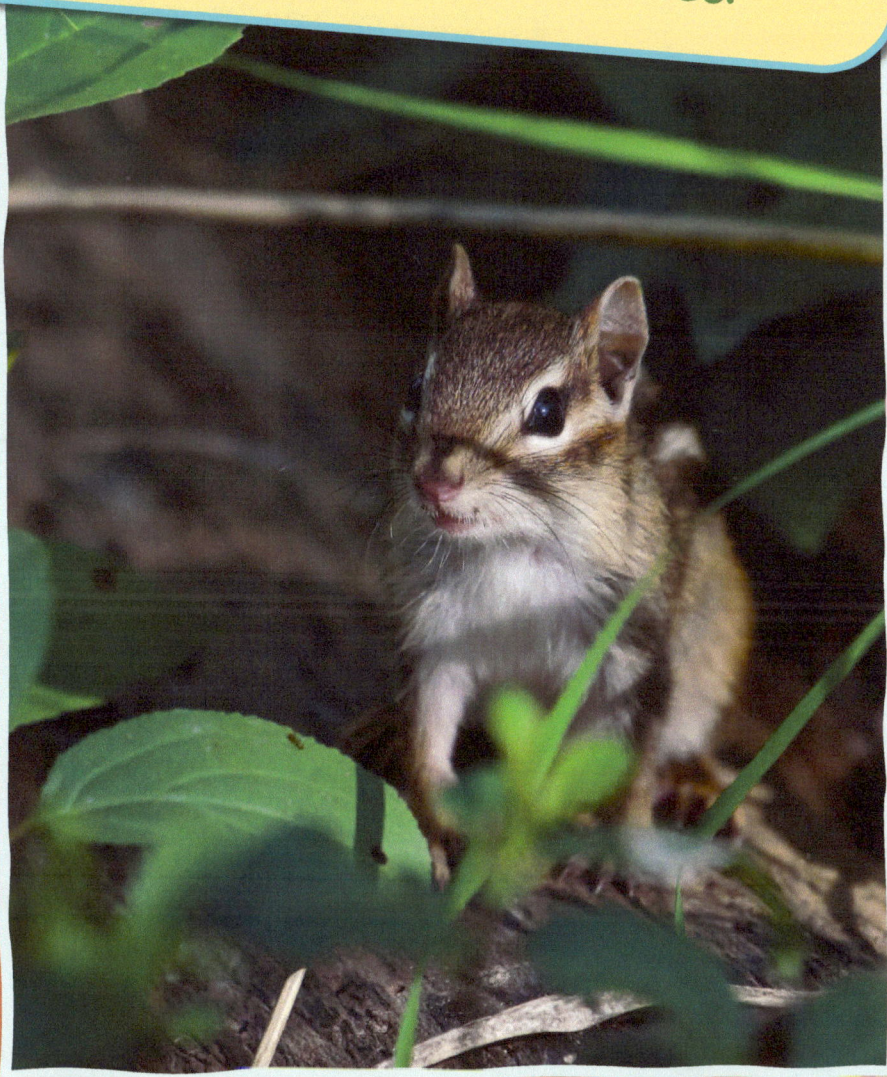

Horned Lizard

North and Central America

The horned lizard lives in dry climates like Arizona, Texas, and Mexico, and it looks like a tasty snack to many predators. But this little lizard has a gruesome defense trick! When hawks, snakes, coyotes or other hunters try to eat it, the horned lizard shoots blood out of ducts in the corners of its eyes. The blood blasts right into the predator's eyes and mouth, stunning them. Then the lizard makes a speedy getaway while its attacker is blinded and grossed out! The blood can shoot up to 4 feet (1.2m), and scientists think it has stuff in it that tastes nasty to coyotes and dogs.

THE HORNED LIZARD SQUIRTS A BLOOD BOMB TO DEFEND ITSELF!

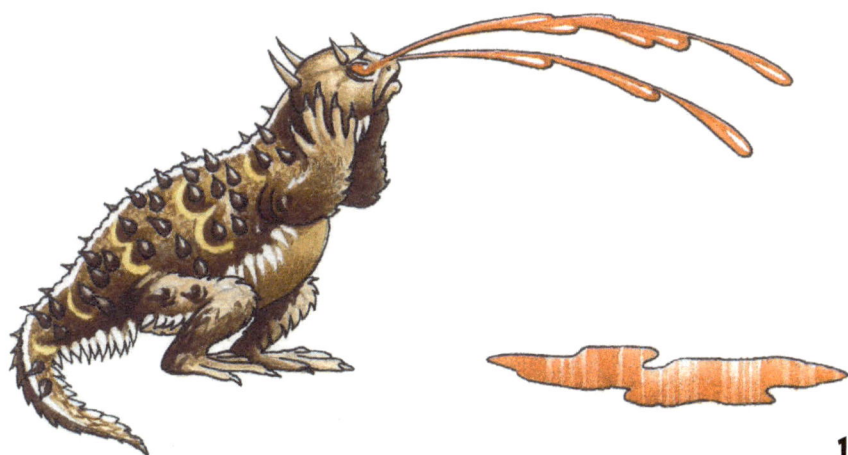

19

Musk Ox

Northern Canada, Greenland, and Alaska

The muskox looks like a giant fluffy stuffed animal. But get close, and you'll smell their horrible stink! These shaggy Arctic beasts use "musk" - smelly urine - to mark territory and attract mates. During mating season, muskox males splash musk all over themselves, drenching their thick, waxy belly fur in the pungent stuff to attract the ladies. The foul stench clings like stinky cologne!

PEE-YEW!

ICKY FACT:

A blue whale can make a fart bubble big enough to fit a horse in it!

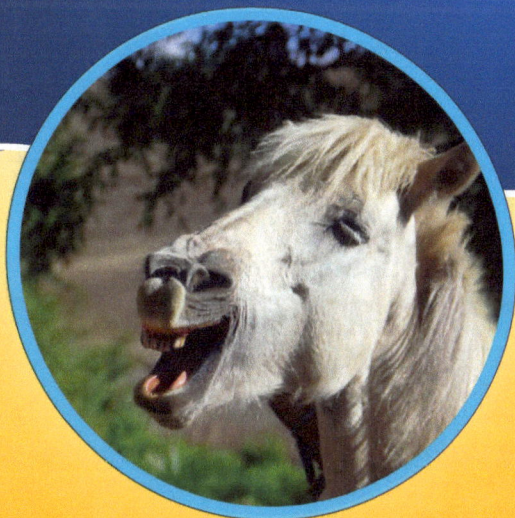

Hairy Frog
Western Africa

If you heard about a frog constantly breaking its own bones, you'd probably think it's pretty clumsy! But the 4-inch hairy frog of West Africa knows exactly what it's doing. This frog uses its skeletal system to turn its feet into stabbing weapons! When threatened, it can flex muscles connected to its hind claws, actually breaking the bones on purpose! Then, the frog pushes the broken bone shards out through the bottom of its feet, using them like weapons. After stabbing its enemy, the bony claws retreat into the frog's feet. Scientists say the tissue around the claws eventually heals.

This frog's crazy self-stabbing move with its own broken bones is so epic; its nickname is the Wolverine frog - like the superhero with blades coming out of his hands!

Sea Cucumber

Across the World

Sea cucumbers move really slowly, so you'd think they'd be super easy for predators to catch. But some kinds have a bizarre defense mechanism! When a predator like a crab attacks, they can shoot their guts - intestines, respiratory system, even reproductive parts - right out of their bottoms. It's true! The predator thinks they look tasty and starts munching away. Meanwhile, the sea cucumber sneaks off to hide under a rock or bury itself in the sand to stay safe.

Recovering after literally popping your guts out is no picnic. The sea cucumber must chill out for a few months, regrowing everything and getting ready to make its next big escape from the next hungry crab hunting for a meal. Pretty grody defense move, right?

ICKY FACT:

Capuchin monkeys pick their noses with sticks! Chimps and gorillas go digging with their fingers, but Capuchins use twigs to mine nose gold instead. Ouch!

Zorilla
Africa

Meet the adorable yet nasty-smelling Zorilla! Also known as the 'striped polecat,' these skunk-like African weasels spray a reeking fluid from their rear ends to repel predators. And it's some powerfully putrid stuff - the stench of burnt hair and sulfur. These stinky weasels are masters at grossing out their enemies. They have potent anal glands that can spray attackers with their disgusting secretions, making them a terrible snack option. One whiff can send predators running in the opposite direction!

ICKY FACT:

Snail slime helps them slide around! Snails ooze slippery mucus from their undersides to cruise by gliding on the goo.

Cockroach

Across the World

Cockroaches aren't just creepy; they spread disease too. These nasty bugs crawl through sewers and garbage, carrying germs on their bodies. They then scurry into homes where they'll contaminate food and surfaces. Cockroaches can spread E. coli, salmonella, dysentery and other gut diseases by walking over food before humans eat it. Their poop and shed skins also trigger asthma. Some cockroaches even bite humans, leaving itchy welts. And the grossness factor? A cockroach will eat about anything - even mucus, skin flakes and toenail clippings! Next time you see one bug, remember it may have dined on someone's dried nose drippings before visiting your kitchen!

COCKROACHES LOVE TO MUNCH ON YOUR HAIR OR FINGERNAILS WHILE YOU'RE SLEEPING! IF THAT DOESN'T GIVE YOU INSOMNIA, NOTHING WILL!

Koala
Australia

Koalas might seem cute, but they have pretty yucky habits! Their diet of eucalyptus leaves has lots of toxins. Adult koalas' stomachs can neutralize the poison, but baby koalas aren't born with that power yet. So what do they eat to prep their tummies? Their mom's poop! *Ick!*

Baby koalas munch on their moms' runny, diarrhea-y poop to get the right gut bacteria they need to be able to eat toxic leaves. It's like the baby koalas get their cootie shots through poop! Some even slurp the poop straight from their mom's stinky butt. Talk about keeping it in the family!

Once their gut is strong enough, young koalas stop eating feces and start munching leaves - toxic substances and all.

ICKY FACT:

Giraffes use their giant tongues to dig for nose nuggets! They go probing way up their nostrils for boogers with their 18-inch-long tongues.

Snot Otter

North America

Meet the snot otter, also known as the eastern hellbender salamander! These slimy amphibians live in rivers across eastern North America, and boy, do they have icky traits! Snot otters secrete tons of thick, sticky mucus all over their bodies - hence the "snot" name. If attacked, this toxic white mucus oozes from their pores and tastes nasty to any hungry predators! Unfortunately, these bizarre creatures are threatened due to pollution and climate change!

Skunk

North and South America

Skunks are too slow to outrun enemies, so they weaponize their stink instead! These black and white creatures spray a mega-nasty mix of sulfur chemicals from tanks under their tails. Their toxic spray blasts with pinpoint accuracy up to 3 meters, and reeks for over a mile!

That's some potent stank power! But skunks try not to overdo it - they only have about 15ml of the nasty juice (enough for 5-8 sprays). It takes a whole week to refill their stink supply!

If a skunk fumigates you with its wretched stench bomb, don't take it personally. Getting a whiff means you're way too close to this farting fink!

33

Hoopoe
Africa, Asia, and Europe

With its punky mohawk feathers, the hoopoe bird might look cute to bird lovers. But get too close, and you'll need nose plugs! These birds have a stink gland near their butts that oozes a disgusting, rotten-flesh-smelling goo all over themselves. It's like the hoopoe's own stinky perfume! The awful stench even repels parasites and germs. Baby hoopoes have their own gross defense - they fart feces right in attackers' faces! So don't be fooled by their cool crest - hoopoes will weaponize their stink and poop to stay safe. Talk about ruffling some feathers!

ICKY FACT:

Platypuses "sweat" milk from their skin to feed their babies! These strange mammals ooze milk from their bodies since they don't have nipples.

Yeti Crab
South Pacific Ocean

Yeti crabs are freaky-looking crabs that live by hot underwater vents deep in the ocean. They grow to about six inches long and are white because sunlight can't reach them down there.

But the weirdest thing about yeti crabs is their super fuzzy, extra-long arms! Why so much hairy fuzz? It's yucky - they use their furry arms to grow bacteria! The warm vent water makes bacteria quickly grow all over the hairs.

Basically, yeti crabs "farm" bacteria on their arms to eat later. **ICK!** So those shaggy limbs aren't to keep warm - they're a bacteria buffet for the yeti crab to snack on.

ICKY FACT:

Rabbits may be adorable, but they have a gross secret: they eat their poop to get more vitamins and nutrients! Rabbits digest food twice by munching their green poo nuggets!

ICKY FACT:

Bonobo monkey parents suck out their babies' boogers! They keep their little ones' nostrils clean by slurping out all the nose nasties. EWWW!

Lesser Anteater
South America

Don't let their cuteness fool you - these anteaters are famous for their potent stink! Their odor is 4-7 times stronger than a skunk's - and that's a top-tier standard for reek!

Also known as the southern tamandua anteater, these anteater species live in South America's forests and grasslands. They usually keep their stench secret. But when threatened, watch out! This critter unleashes a wretched stink blast so horrible it can clear out a building.

Next to these stench-packing creatures, skunks smell as fresh as daisies!

Hoatzin

South America

Meet the hoatzin, also nicknamed the "Stink Bird." This tropical bird lives in the Amazon and Orinoco Delta in South America. So, how did it get its not-so-charming nickname? Blame the hoatzin's diet and digestion.

The hoatzin is the only bird that eats mostly leaves. It uses fermentation in its gut to break down all that plant matter. The smell produced by this process mixes with the chemicals in the leaves themselves, creating a foul, manure-like stench!

So, while most birds munch on worms or seeds, the hoatzin feasts on vegetation. But the stink bird's leafy diet gives it breath so bad; you'll wish you had a clothespin for your nose! No wonder they came up with the nickname Stink Bird!

Honey Badger
Africa and Asia

The 30-pound honey badger has earned the title of the world's most fearless animal. It's willing to fight animals way bigger than itself and is not afraid to take on a lion or buffalo. This little beast has more than a super strong jaw and thick, tough skin to defend itself. It also has a sickening trick - it can turn the pouch on its rear end inside out and spray enemies with a stinky, suffocating stench! This musky stink bomb spray sends predators running away. You'd probably do the same thing if someone you just met pulled that smelly trick on you!

Honey Badgers usually live alone. I can't imagine why.

ICKY FACT:

Never eat food shared by a rat!
Rats can't vomit, so poisons can kill them. So, how do rats let their friends know there's something good to eat? Well, they pee on safe foods, so other rats know it's okay to eat. Uh, yum?

Botfly

Central and South America

Botflies unleash their skin-burrowing terror through mosquitoes. First, a pregnant botfly attaches her eggs to a mosquito. When the bloodsucker bites a person, the eggs hatch, and the tiny larvae crawl into your skin through the bite. For 6-10 weeks, the maggot lives embedded under your skin, using rear hooks to hang on. You might even see its snout poking out as it breathes! Eventually, the larva pops out, leaving a quarter-sized hole behind. *YIKES!*

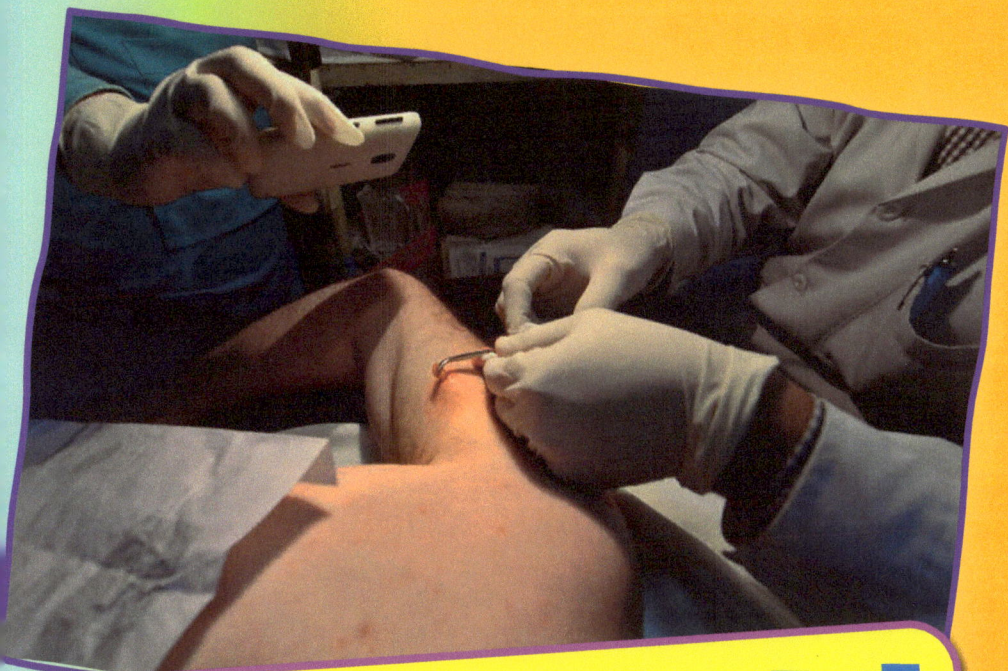

KEEP AN EYE ON ANY MOSQUITO BITE THAT DOESN'T HEAL - YOU MIGHT HATCH A BOTFLY!

Dung Beetle

Across the World

Dung beetles are all about rolling and eating poop! These inch-long beetles live all over the world and feed on the feces of animals like elephants, cows, and horses. Using their mouthparts, they shape dung into little balls. Then, they roll the balls away using their back legs, often working in teams. Why make poop balls? Female dung beetles lay their eggs inside the dung balls to feed their babies! The eggs hatch into worm-like larvae that eat all the poop. After becoming pupae, the beetles emerge from the balls as adults to repeat the process.

Can you imagine being born and living in a ball of animal poop? Yuck! But for dung beetles, that's home sweet home.

ICKY FACT:

Bush babies, also called galagoes, pee on their paws so they don't get lost! Their urine helps them grip branches and marks their way home.

Tongue Louse

Atlantic and Pacific Oceans

The tongue louse is a sneaky parasite that invades a fish's mouth. First, this creepy crustacean enters through the gills. Using hooked claws, it attaches to the base of the tongue. Clamped on tight, the louse feeds on the fish's blood and any loose food particles swallowed. Over time, they nibble away at the tongue until only a tiny stump is left behind! But the parasite keeps feeding as if the whole tongue was still there. The oblivious fish never realizes the teeny invader is feasting inside its mouth! Pretty wild how the tiny louse fools the fish into letting it eat away at its tongue!

Tongue louses start in life as male. But later on, they turn into females! These creatures are "protandrous hermaphrodites," which means they change from male to female as they get older.

Eurasian Roller
Africa, Europe, and Asia

Picture this - you see some people you want to say hello to. But as you get closer, they barf all over you! Disgusting, right? You'd probably want to stay far away from them after that. Young Eurasian roller birds do something similar for a good reason. They travel from Europe to Asia, and on the way, they meet lots of snakes, rats, and predators that might eat them. When the baby birds spit up their gross, orange, stinky stomach fluid, it keeps the predators away. It also alerts their parents that there's danger nearby. So even though it's rude and revolting, the baby birds are just trying to defend themselves on their long journey by hurling vomit at anything that seems scary!

ICKY FACT:

The marine iguana sneezes out salty snot! Special glands remove excess salt from these lizards' noses. Then they blast it out in mega snot rockets!

Turkey Vulture

North, Central, and South America

The creepy-looking Turkey vulture is relatively harmless, but its dinner choices are nauseating! This vulture loves to eat dead, decaying animals and roadkill. When vultures finally get to eat a rotting carcass, it can be full of toxic stuff that would kill other scavengers. But vultures' strong stomach acid lets them eat diseased carcasses without getting sick. They stuff themselves so full their throat sacks bulge out. If a predator spooks them, they barf up the food so they can fly away!

As if that wasn't gross enough, there's also an interesting reason these vultures don't have feathers on their heads and necks. Turkey vultures are bald, so they can shove their heads deep into dead bodies without getting gunk stuck in feathers!

VULTURES MAY SEEM NASTY, BUT THEIR HABITS HELP THEM SAFELY EAT ROTTING MEAT AND FEND OFF PREDATORS!

Ornate Narrow-Mouthed Frog
Asia

The ornate, narrow-mouthed frog is a teensy 1-inch-long amphibian that lives in Asia's forests and grasslands. But don't let its size fool you - this frog has a big appetite for finding food in elephant poop! Yep, it happily makes smelly dung piles its home.

Why live in a giant mound of stinky elephant poop? For one, it offers shelter from the hot sun. But the main benefit is the 24/7 poop buffet! The frog feasts on the insects crawling all over the dung. When bugs are scarce, it just chomps down on leftover chunks of undigested food inside the poop.

If you think frogs are all lily pads and fly-eating, think again! For the ornate narrow-mouthed frog, it's all about living large in elephant poop, and snacking on bugs and leftovers in the ultimate rotten restaurant.

ICKY FACT:

The South American degu can see ultraviolet light and uses its pee as a lighted map! Its UV-reflecting urine lights up passageways in its burrow, letting the degu find its way home.

Surinam Toad

South America

Toads aren't known for looking good. But the Surinam toad is especially ugly – a mushy, flat blob with googly eyes that blends in with wet leaves. What's really nasty, though, is how Surinam toads reproduce.

When they mate, the male and female do a long, swirling dance in the water. After that, the female releases about 100 eggs for the male to fertilize. That's where things get freaky. The male sticks the fertilized eggs right onto the female's back! Then, the female grows a thick layer of skin over the eggs, trapping them there.

The eggs turn into full baby toads inside the mom's back. Finally, the babies burst out through her skin, leaving behind holes where they popped out. The babies swim away, while the mom is left with a back full of birth holes. **Ouch!**

Tapeworm
Across the World

Tapeworms are nasty parasites that can live in many animals, including humans. These worm-like creatures latch onto the intestinal wall using hooks or suckers on their head. Tapeworms grow by forming segment after segment in their bodies. Mature segments filled with eggs break off and exit the host through feces. If the poor infected person doesn't wash their hands well enough, they can accidentally swallow the tapeworm eggs and reinfect themselves! The cycle repeats as the tapeworm keeps growing and shedding more egg-filled segments. A person can end up with a 30-foot-long tapeworm made of 1000 segments inside them!

ICKY FACT:

Kangaroos lick themselves to stay cool! The spit helps lower their body temperature as it evaporates.

Bombardier Beetle

Across the World

The bombardier beetle isn't kidding around with its name - it does bomb its enemies! This half-inch-long beetle defends itself by shooting hot, burning chemicals at anything that attacks it. Inside the beetle, there are two glands. One gland has chemicals called hydrogen peroxide and hydroquinone, and the other gland has special enzymes. When the beetle mixes the contents of the two glands, the combination reaches 212 degrees F - that's as hot as boiling water! Then, the beetle shoots the burning mixture from a super accurate nozzle-like opening on its rear end. It can blast its hot chemicals up to 20 times in a row before running out.

Don't mess with the bombardier beetle, or you'll get bombed!

The chemicals are hot enough to burn human skin!

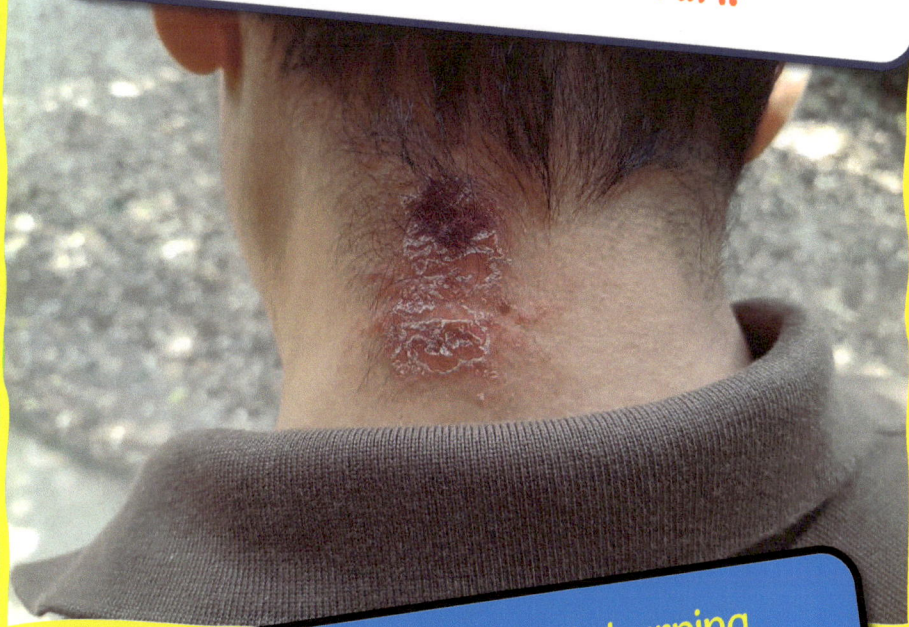

As if getting blasted with burning chemicals wasn't bad enough, this beetle's liquid weapon is also super stinky!

Maggot
Across the World

Maggots are the wriggling baby flies that hatch from fly eggs. What's so disgusting about maggots? For one, they eat rotten, decaying things. Maggots feast on dead stuff, like garbage and roadkill. They use sharp little hooks in their mouths to tear and slurp up yucky decaying flesh and liquids. To make more maggots, flies lay their eggs inside rotten food, wounds, and even animals' noses! Then the eggs hatch into slimy white maggot babies that squirm all over, eating and pooping everywhere. When they get bigger, the maggots turn into flies and fly off to lay more eggs. Pretty nasty, right?

ICKY FACT:

The California sheephead fish coats itself in mucus! At night, these fish blanket their bodies in the slimy goop so predators can't detect them.

INDEX

Enjoy these other great books in the Wonderful World of Animals Series by JACK LEWIS:

The Cutest Animals of the World Book for Kids

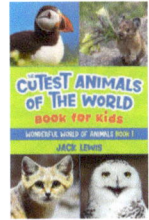

The Weirdest Animals of the World Book for Kids

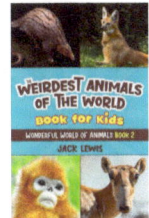

Dangerous Animals of the World Book for Kids

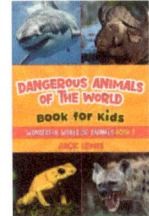

Funny Animals of the World Joke Book for Kids

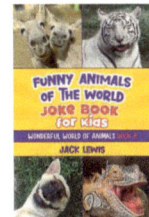

The Grossest Animal Facts Ever Book for Kids

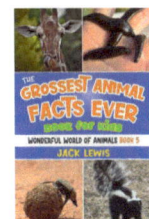